D030551Z

DISCOVER THE NIGHT SKY

EXPLORING
ECLIPSES

BY JILL SHERMAN

Consultant:
Ilia Iankov Roussev, PhD

raintree

a Capstone company — publishers for children

Raintree is an imprint of Capstone Global Library Limited, a company incorporated in England and
Wales having its registered office at 264 Banbury Road, Oxford, OX2 7DY – Registered company
number: 6695582

www.raintree.co.uk
myorders@raintree.co.uk

Text © Capstone Global Library Limited 2018
The moral rights of the proprietor have been asserted.

ISBN 978 1 4747 4992 3
22 21 20 19 18 17
10 9 8 7 6 5 4 3 2 1

Editorial Credits
Adrian Vigliano, editor; Veronica Scott, designer;
Wanda Winch, media researcher; Gene Bentdahl, production specialist

BRENT LIBRARIES

91120000341407	
Askews & Holts	06-Sep-2017
J523.99	£12.99

A full catalogue record for this book is available from the British Library.

Acknowledgements
We would like to thank the following for permission to reproduce photographs: Alamy Stock Photo:
Hemis, 23 (bottom), Ivy Close Images, 7 (top), Photo Researchers, Inc., 21 (b); Dreamstime: Astrobobo,
18–19, Igorfp, 28; iStockphoto: adventtr, 8–9; Newscom: Reuters/David Gray, 26–27; Science Source:
Claus Lunau, 25; Shutterstock: BlueRingMedia, 11, Chiradech Chotchaung, 29, Dr. Ajay Kumar Singh,
10, Georgios Kollidas, 7 (b), Igor Zh., cover, NikoNomad, 22–23 (background), Pavel Vakhrushev,
starfield background, Pi-Lens, 5, Tom Tietz, 13 (bottom right), Viliam.M, 16–17 (background);
Thinkstock: iStockphoto/demarfa, 21 (t), iStockphoto/NdRphotographer, 17 (b), iStockphoto/SMJoness,
12–13 (background), iStockphoto/solarseven, 15

All rights reserved. No part of this publication may be reproduced in any form or by any means
(including photocopying or storing it in any medium by electronic means and whether or not
transiently or incidentally to some other use of this publication) without the written permission of
the copyright owner, except in accordance with the provisions of the Copyright, Designs and Patents
Act 1988 or under the terms of a licence issued by the Copyright Licensing Agency, Saffron House,
6–10 Kirby Street, London EC1N 8TS (www.cla.co.uk). Applications for the copyright owner's written
permission should be addressed to the publisher.

Every effort has been made to contact copyright holders of material reproduced in this book. Any
omissions will be rectified in subsequent printings if notice is given to the publisher.

All the Internet addresses (URLs) given in this book were valid at the time of going to press. However,
due to the dynamic nature of the Internet, some addresses may have changed sites may have
changed or ceased to exist since publication. While the author and publisher regret any inconvenience
this may cause readers, no responsibility for any such changes can be accepted by either the author or
the publisher.

Printed and bound in China.

CHAPTER 1

WHAT IS AN ECLIPSE?

The night sky is full of stars. You can see the Moon and sometimes other planets too. They may look still, but these objects are in constant motion. As Earth moves through space, new objects come into view. Others are blocked.

When one object in space moves into the shadow of another, it is called an **eclipse**. The second object is no longer totally visible. It is still there. It is just hiding in shadow.

The most common eclipses that we see are of the Sun and Moon. Earth **orbits** the Sun, and the Moon orbits Earth. When their orbits align, they cast shadows. The shadows create an eclipse. It is a stunning event to see.

eclipse – when one object in space blocks light and keeps it from shining on another object in space

orbit – path an object follows as it goes around the Sun or a planet

FIRST RECORDS

Ancient peoples watched the Sun, Moon and stars. They used the movements to make calendars. When these objects seemed to disappear, it was an important event. The earliest records of eclipses were made in China. They date back more than 4,000 years. Chinese scientists studied the patterns. This helped them to predict future eclipses.

Still, the cause of an eclipse was a mystery. They became part of **mythology**. Norse tribes believed a giant wolf ate the Sun during an eclipse. Hindus described serpents that sucked away the Sun's light.

Eclipses were also considered a bad omen. Ancient Greeks believed it meant a disaster was coming. It was also a bad sign for rulers. In Babylon, fake kings were put on the throne during eclipses. This was meant to protect the real rulers from harm.

Did you know?

In AD 1133 there was an eclipse. King Henry I died shortly afterwards. The eclipse lasted 4 minutes and 38 seconds. It's known as King Henry's Eclipse. The king's death seemed like a clear sign that eclipses meant danger.

King Henry I

CHAPTER 2

WHEN DOES AN ECLIPSE OCCUR?

Eclipses are not common events. Earth and the Moon cast shadows into space as they make their orbit. On Earth we can't usually see the shadows. We can only see the shadows when objects such as the Sun, Earth and Moon cross paths in a straight line.

Sometimes the Moon passes directly between Earth and the Sun. The Moon blocks the light from the Sun. It casts a shadow on Earth. For people standing in the shadow, the Sun has been blocked out. The area passes into darkness. This event is called a **solar eclipse**. The Sun is blocked out from view.

At other times, Earth will pass directly between the Sun and Moon. Earth blocks sunlight from reaching the Moon. This blocks the Moon. This event is a **lunar eclipse**.

solar eclipse – astronomical event in which the Moon passes between the Sun and Earth
lunar eclipse – astronomical event in which Earth's shadow passes over the Moon

LUNAR ECLIPSES

A lunar eclipse happens only during the night of a full Moon. On these nights the entire face of the Moon is lit. Then Earth passes between the Sun and the Moon. Earth eclipses the Moon. Its shadow covers the Moon.

There are two types of lunar eclipses – total and partial. In a partial eclipse, the Sun, Earth and Moon are almost, but not perfectly, in line. Only part of the Moon enters Earth's shadow. A dark shadow passes over the Moon's surface.

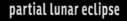

partial lunar eclipse

For a total eclipse, the Sun, Earth and Moon are in a perfect line. The Moon is entirely within Earth's shadow. But the Moon does not go completely dark. Some sunlight still reaches the Moon.

Sun

Earth

Moon

Sunlight is made up of different types of light. It contains all the colours of the rainbow. Light from the Sun passes through Earth's atmosphere, which acts like a lens. The air bends the light. It separates into different colours. Red light bends. Some of it reaches the Moon. So the Moon takes on a red colour during an eclipse.

The exact colour of the Moon during an eclipse can change a little. Temperature, humidity or a recent volcanic eruption can change how the light bends. This is the same reason that some sunsets vary in shades of red, orange and gold. In an eclipse, the Moon may show shades of red, orange, gold or pink.

Usually, a lunar eclipse lasts for a few hours. There are about two partial eclipses every year. Total lunar eclipses occur about once every 18 months. They are visible wherever it's night-time on Earth.

Did you know?

A lunar eclipse is often called a "blood moon". In ancient times a blood moon was often seen as a bad omen. It was thought to signal the end of the world.

SOLAR ECLIPSES

When the Moon comes between Earth and the Sun, it blocks out the Sun's light. The Moon eclipses the Sun. A shadow is cast on Earth. A solar eclipse occurs. Solar eclipses occur about every 18 months. They last only a few minutes. Solar eclipses are visible only in a narrow path on Earth's surface. The path is less than 300 kilometres (186 miles) wide. There are three types of solar eclipses. They are total, partial and annular eclipses.

A total eclipse can only be seen from a small area on Earth. The people in that place see the Moon's shadow. The shadow hits Earth, blocking out sunlight. The Sun is completely covered. The sky gets dark. Only a thin halo of light peeks out from behind the Moon. The Sun, Moon and Earth must be exactly in line for a total eclipse to occur.

A partial eclipse happens when the Sun, Moon and Earth are almost lined up. The Moon covers part of the Sun. The Sun looks like a crescent. It looks like someone has taken a bite out of it.

During an annular eclipse, the Moon passes directly in front of the Sun. But it does not cover the Sun completely. Sometimes the Moon's orbit takes it closer to Earth than others. Sometimes it is further away. When the Moon is closer, it looks larger. It can cover the entire Sun. When the Moon is further away, it looks smaller. It does not block the whole Sun. A dark circle covers the centre of the Sun. A bright ring glows around the dark centre.

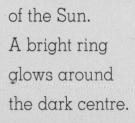

partial solar eclipse

PARTS OF THE ECLIPSE

During a solar eclipse, the Moon casts two shadows on Earth. The first shadow is the umbra. It gets smaller as it reaches Earth. The umbra is the dark centre of the Moon's shadow. Sunlight is completely blocked.

The second shadow is the penumbra. This shadow gets larger as it reaches Earth. It surrounds the umbra. Sunlight is partly blocked. It casts a lighter shadow.

Only a small area of Earth falls in the umbra of an eclipse. The area is just 300 kilometres (186 miles) wide. The shadow sweeps across Earth's surface. It travels west to east. People in the shade of the umbra will see a total eclipse. People in the penumbra will see a partial eclipse.

A solar eclipse has two shadows: umbra and penumbra

penumbra

umbra

OTHER ECLIPSES

Not all eclipses are of the Sun, Moon and Earth. Two planets come between Earth and the Sun. They are Mercury and Venus. The planets form an eclipse called a transit. They travel across the face of the Sun. From Earth the planets look like small black dots. Transits are very rare. Over a span of 100 years, there are only about 13 transits of Mercury. During that time Venus transits just twice.

Astronomers also observe eclipses on other planets. Jupiter and its moons have lunar and solar eclipses. When a moon or planet blocks light from a distant star that is also an eclipse. Any type of eclipse can help scientists to better understand space.

astronomer – scientist who studies stars, planets and other objects in space

Venus transit

The speed of light

In 1675 Olaus Roemer was studying eclipses on Jupiter. He measured how long the eclipses lasted. A moon would disappear behind Jupiter. But it did not always take the same time to reappear. Roemer found that the time depended on how close Earth was to Jupiter. The time difference showed that light travelled with speed. He calculated the speed of light. It moves very fast. Light travels at 299,792 kilometres (186,000 miles) per second.

CHAPTER 3

ECLIPSE SCIENCE

Eclipses give scientists a unique look at the night sky. Every eclipse lets them learn more. Space agencies around the world study eclipses. In the United States that agency is NASA.

In 2011, NASA sent an **orbiter** to study an eclipse. It measured the change in the Moon's temperature. This helped scientists to work out what the Moon's surface is made of. They also learned about the terrain. Smooth surfaces cool more quickly. Rough surfaces take longer to cool.

During a solar eclipse, NASA studies the Sun's **corona**. This is the Sun's outer atmosphere. It is very faint. It is only visible during an eclipse. Scientists hope to learn how the corona affects Earth.

Coronagraph

Scientists are very interested in the corona. But waiting for a solar eclipse takes a long time. That is why scientists created the coronagraph. It is a special type of telescope. It mimics a solar eclipse. Now scientists can view the corona at any time. The device also has other uses. Today, they are used to discover far away **exoplanets**.

orbiter - spacecraft that orbits a planet or other space objects
corona - outermost part of the Sun's atmosphere
exoplanet - planet that orbits a star outside the solar system

DISCOVERIES FROM ECLIPSES

Solar eclipses have led to some great discoveries. During an 1868 eclipse, scientists saw a yellow line in the Sun's spectrum. It was not made by any known **element**. They named the new element after the ancient-Greek god of the Sun, Helios. Helium is the second lightest element. It is very common, but scientists did not know it existed until the eclipse allowed them to see it!

In 1915, Albert Einstein wrote his **theory** of relativity. It is his most famous work. He said that light from faraway stars bends when it passes by the Sun. The Sun is too bright for us to see the passing starlight. But it can be photographed during a solar eclipse. During an eclipse in 1919 scientists took photos of the starlight. It bent! Einstein was right.

element – basic substance in chemistry that cannot be split into simpler substances
theory – idea that brings together several hypotheses to explain something

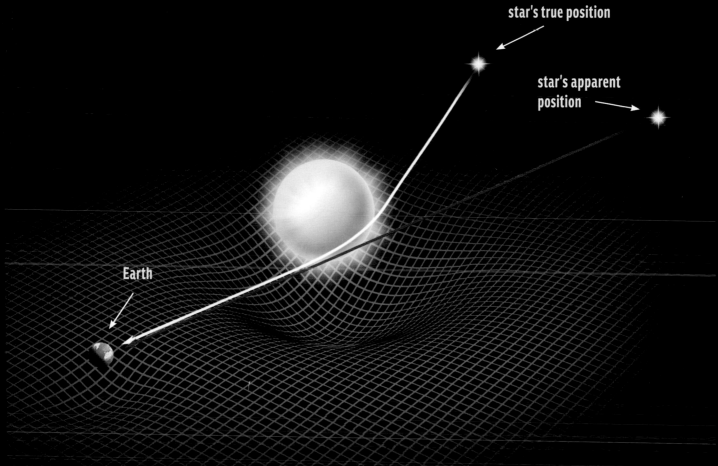

star's true position

star's apparent position

Earth

Coordinated observations

Scientists continue to study eclipses. They can learn more by working together. Scientists take photographs at the same time from many locations. Then they compare the data. They look at how it has changed over time. This helps them to learn about changes in the Sun and Moon.

CHAPTER 4

PREDICTING ECLIPSES

Scientists know the paths that Earth and the Moon travel. They also know the speeds of the orbits. Using this data, they predict when and where future eclipses will occur.

Earth sees several eclipses each year. NASA knows about all future eclipses until the year 3000. The dates are posted on NASA's website. Anyone can check the calendar. You can find out where to go to watch Earth's next eclipse.

SELECTED ECLIPSE CALENDAR

DATE	TYPE OF ECLIPSE	PLACES WHERE IT WILL BE VISIBLE
11 Aug 2018	partial solar	North/East Europe, North/West Asia, North America, Atlantic Ocean, Arctic
20 Jan/21 Jan 2019	total lunar	Europe, Asia, Africa, North America, South America, Pacific Ocean, Atlantic Ocean, Indian Ocean, Arctic
2 Jul 2019	total solar	North America, much of South America, Pacific Ocean
11 Nov 2019	Mercury transit	South/West Europe, South/West Asia, Africa, much of North America, South America, Indian Ocean, Antarctica
26 Dec 2019	annular solar	East in Europe, much of Asia, North/West Australia, East in Africa, Pacific Ocean, Indian Ocean
26 May 2021	total lunar	South/East Asia, Australia, much of North America, South America, Pacific Ocean, Atlantic Ocean, Indian Ocean, Antarctica
25 Oct 2022	partial solar	Europe, South/West Asia, North/East Africa, Atlantic Ocean

VIEWING AN ECLIPSE

Watching an eclipse is an exciting event. But it cannot be seen from just anywhere. Your part of the planet may not have an eclipse for many years. When one happens in your area, it is a historic event.

Lunar eclipses are easy to watch. You can see them with the naked eye. But you may want to use a telescope. It will allow you to see the eclipse in more detail. You could also find a local planetarium and see if an eclipse viewing will be hosted there.

Solar eclipses are more difficult. You should never look directly at the Sun. Doing so could damage your eyes. It could even cause blindness.

Most people watch a solar eclipse using special glasses or a cardboard viewer. An eclipse viewer has a small hole cut into it. Sunlight shines through the hole and onto a surface. During an eclipse, the Moon's shadow moves across this ray of light. With the right tools, you can safely watch your next eclipse.

GLOSSARY

astronomer   scientist who studies stars, planets and other objects in space

corona   outermost part of the Sun's atmosphere

eclipse   when one object in space blocks light and keeps it from shining on another object in space

element   basic substance in chemistry that cannot be split into simpler substances

exoplanet   planet that orbits a star outside the solar system

lunar eclipse   astronomical event in which Earth's shadow passes over the Moon

mythology   old or ancient stories told again and again that help connect people with their past

orbit   path an object follows as it goes around the Sun or a planet

orbiter   spacecraft that orbits a planet or other space objects

solar eclipse   astronomical event in which the Moon passes between the Sun and Earth

theory   idea that brings together several hypotheses to explain something

READ MORE

Eclipses (The Night Sky: and Other Amazing Sights), Nick Hunter (Raintree, 2013)

The Moon (Astronaut Travel Guides), Chris Oxlade (Raintree, 2013)

Space: Visual Encyclopedia, DK (DK Publishing, 2016)

WEBSITES

www.dkfindout.com/uk/space/solar-system/
Find out more about the solar system.

www.esa.int/esaKIDSen/
Learn more from the European Space Agency.

COMPREHENSION QUESTIONS

1. What is the difference between a lunar and solar eclipse?

2. Why do scientists study eclipses?

3. If Earth had no atmosphere, what colour would the Moon be during a lunar eclipse?

INDEX